POSTERS
OF
WORLD WARS I AND II
CD-ROM and Book

DOVER PUBLICATIONS, INC.
Mineola, New York

The CD-ROM in this book contains all of the images. Each image is offered in two sizes on the CD – approximately 4½" by 6½", and approximately 7" by 10". Each image has been scanned at 300 dpi and saved in high quality JPEG format. There is no installation necessary. Just insert the CD into your computer and call the images into your favorite software (refer to the documentation with your software for further instructions).

All of the graphics files are in the Images folder on the CD. Every image has a unique file name in the following format: xxx.JPG. The first 3 digits of the file name correspond to the number printed under the image in the book. The last 3 letters of the file name, "JPG," refer to the file format. So, 001.JPG would be the first file in the Images folder.

Also included on the CD-ROM is Dover Design Manager, a simple graphics editing program for Windows that will allow you to view, print, crop, and rotate the images.

For technical support, contact:
Telephone: 1 (617) 249-0245
Fax: 1 (617) 249-0245
Email: dover@artimaging.com
Internet: **http://www.dovertechsupport.com**
The fastest way to receive technical support is via email or the Internet.

002. CHARLES LIVINGSTON BULL, C. 1917

001. JAMES MONTGOMERY FLAGG, 1917

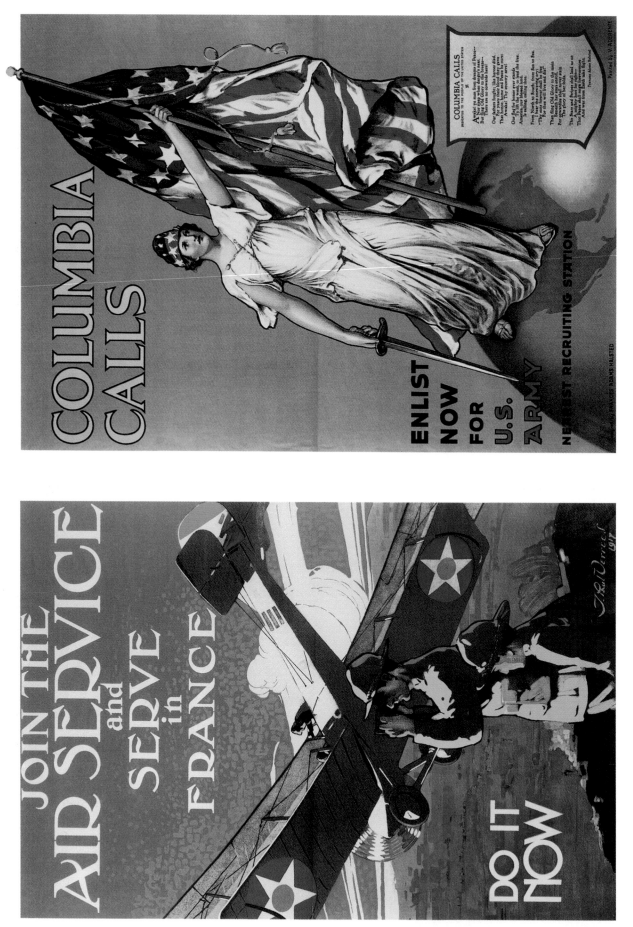

004. Francis Adams Halstead and V. Aderante, 1916

003. J. Paul Verrees, 1917

006. SIDNEY H. REISENBERG, C. 1917

005. JAMES MONTGOMERY FLAGG, C. 1918

008. James Montgomery Flagg, 1917

007. James Montgomery Flagg, c. 1918

010. Howard Chandler Christy, 1918

009. Howard Chandler Christy, 1915

012. Kenyon Cox, c. 1917

011. Charles Dana Gibson, 1917

014. August Hutof, c. 1918

013. Joseph Christian Leyendecker, 1917

016. LAURA BREY, 1917

015. FRED SPEAR, 1915

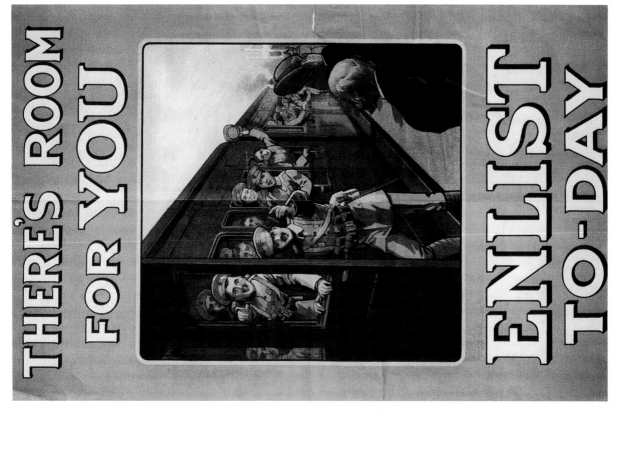

THERE'S ROOM FOR YOU

ENLIST TO-DAY

018. W. A. FRY, C. 1915

Something doing boys!
Uncle Sams on the bridge

ENLIST

Issued by The City of Boston Public Safety Committee

017. ARTIST UNKNOWN, C. 1917

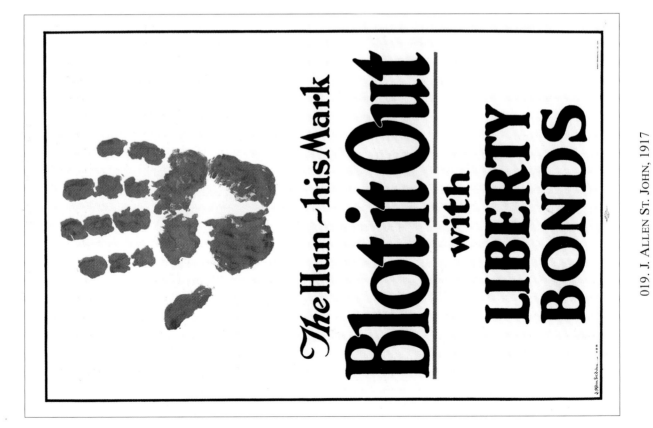

020. Fred Strothman, 1918

019. J. Allen St. John, 1917

022. G. R. MACAULEY, 1917

021. WALTER WHITEHEAD, 1918

024. John Norton, 1918

023. Henry Patrick Raleigh, 1918

026. R. H. PORTEUS, 1917

025. DAN SAYRE GROESBECK, 1917

028. SIDNEY H. REISENBERG, 1918

027. ARTIST UNKNOWN, 1917

030. Joseph Christian Leyendecker, 1918

029. Howard Chandler Christy, 1917

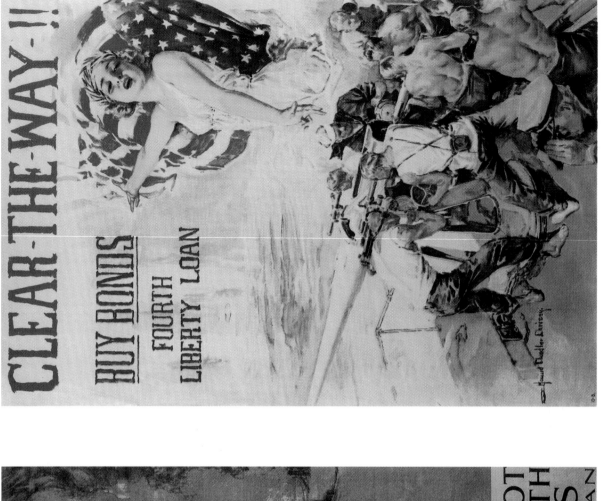

032. HOWARD CHANDLER CHRISTY, 1918

031. JOSEPH PENNELL, 1918

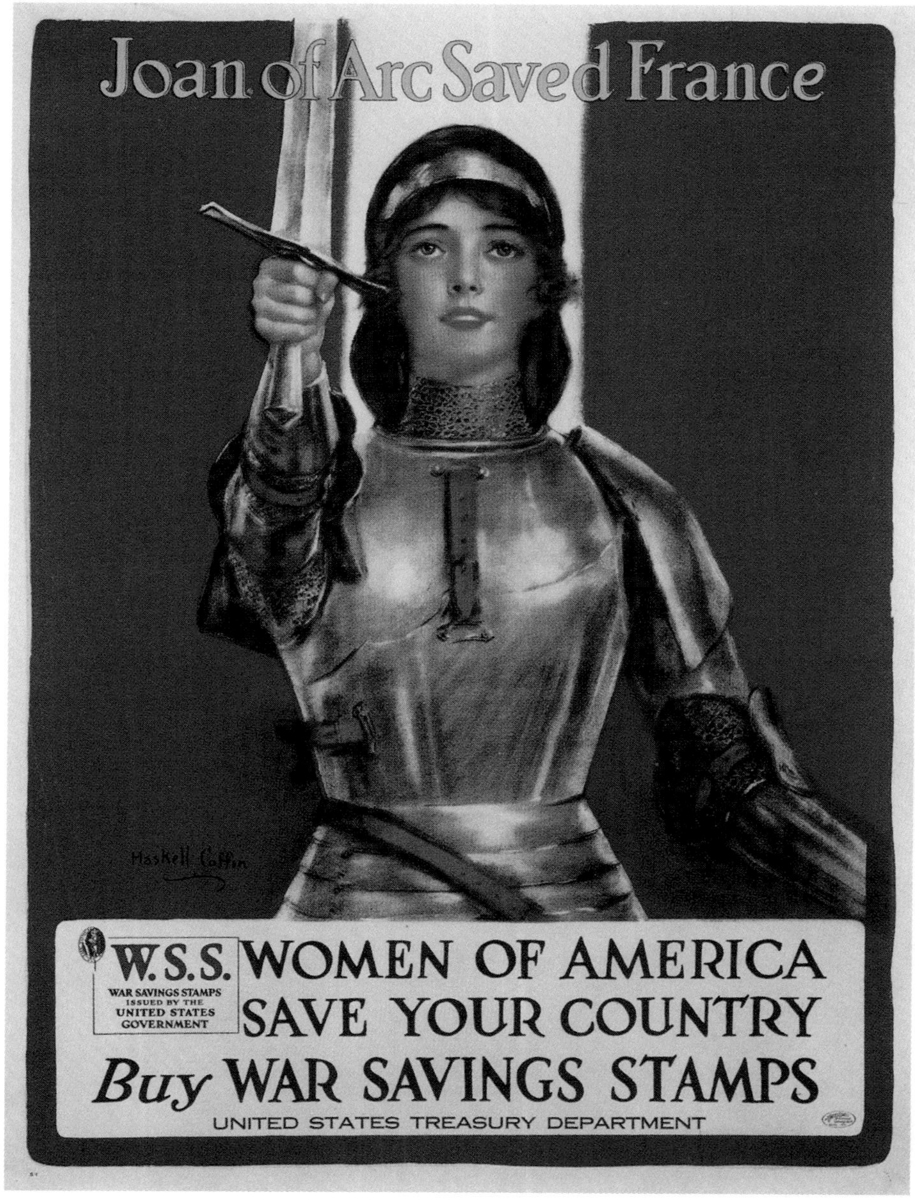

033. HASKELL COFFIN, 1918

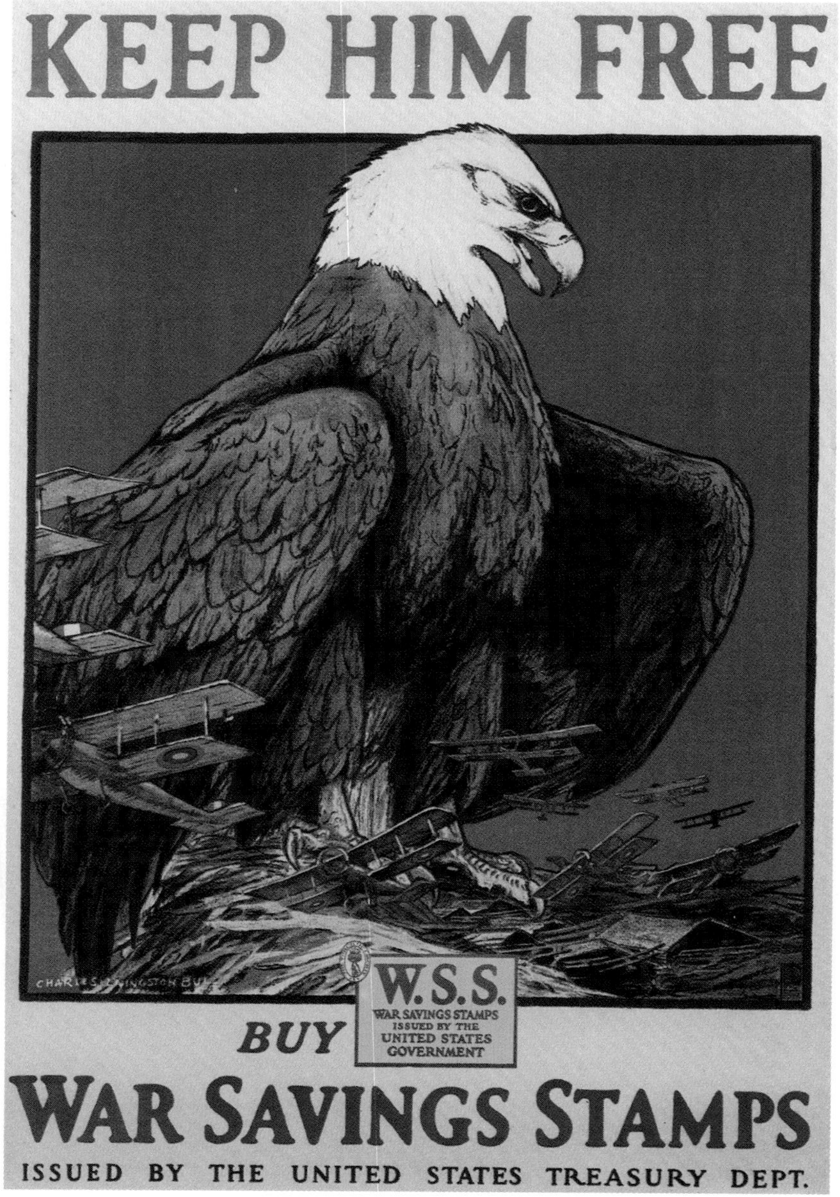

034. CHARLES LIVINGSTON BULL, 1918

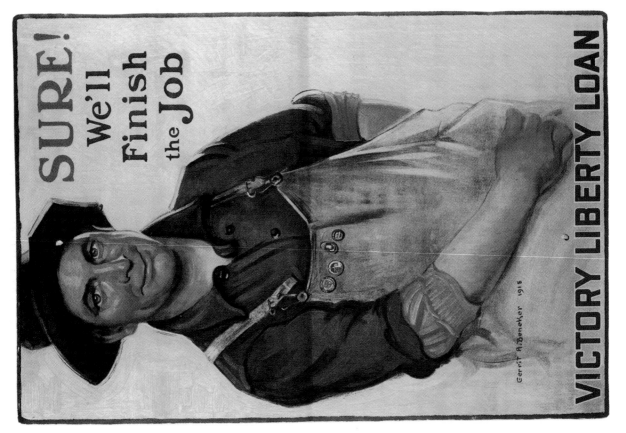

036. GERRIT A. BENEKER, 1918

035. HOWARD CHANDLER CHRISTY, 1919

038. HARRISON FISHER, 1918

037. ALONZO EARL FORINGER, C. 1918

040. Edwin Howland Blashfield, c. 1918

039. Howard Chandler Christy, 1919

042. MACINEL WRIGHT ENRIGHT, C. 1919

041. ARTIST UNKNOWN, C. 1918

044. Charles E. Chambers, 1917

043. John E. Sheridan, c. 1918

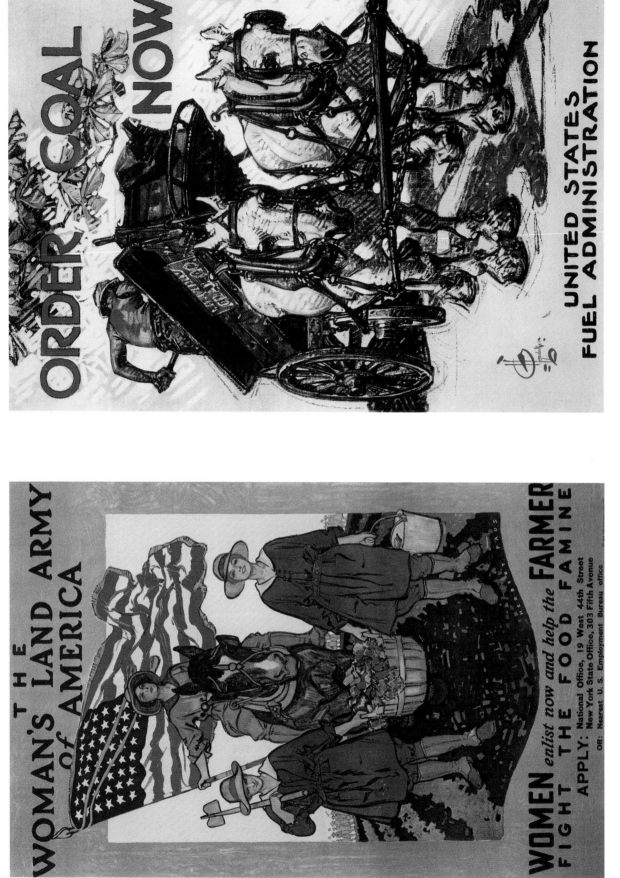

046. Joseph Christian Leyendecker, c. 1918

045. Herbert Andrew Paus, 1918

048. James Montgomery Flagg, 1917

047. James Montgomery Flagg, 1917

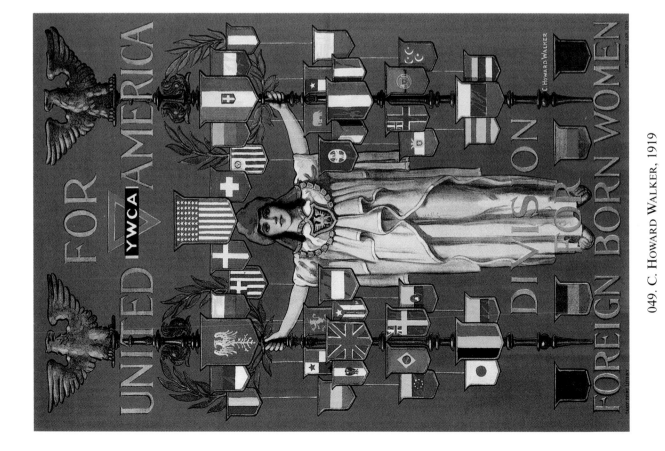

049. C. Howard Walker, 1919

050. Artist Unknown, c. 1916

052. ETHEL FRANKLIN BETTS BAINS, C. 1917

051. PAUL HONORÉ, C. 1917

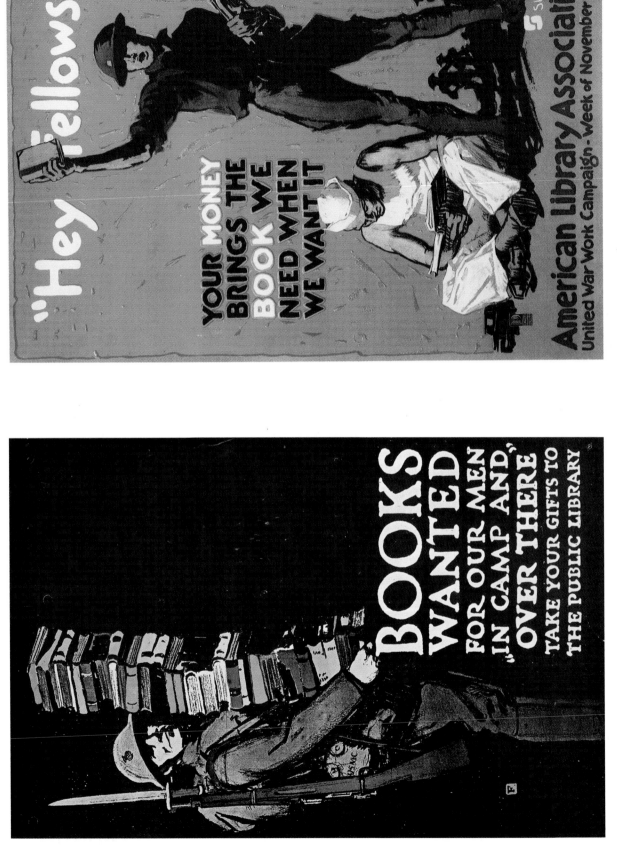

054. JOHN E. SHERIDAN, 1918

053. CHARLES BUCKLES FALLS, C. 1918

Help him to help U.S.!

Help the
Horse to
Save the
Soldier

THE AMERICAN **RED STAR** ANIMAL RELIEF

National Headquarters, Albany, N.Y.

056. James Montgomery Flagg, c. 1918

Have YOU a
Red Cross Service Flag?

1918

055. Jesse Willcox Smith, 1918

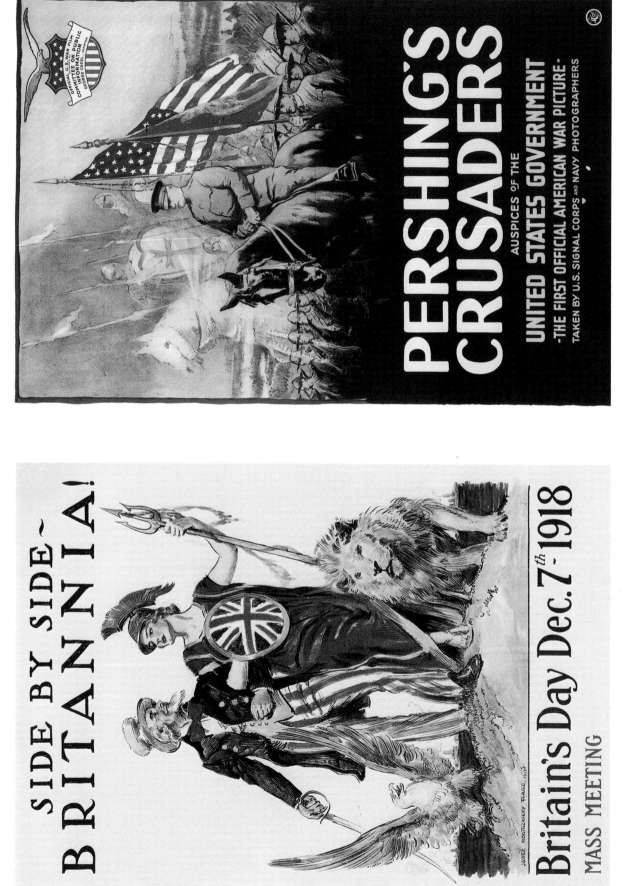

058. Artist Unknown, 1918

057. James Montgomery Flagg, 1918

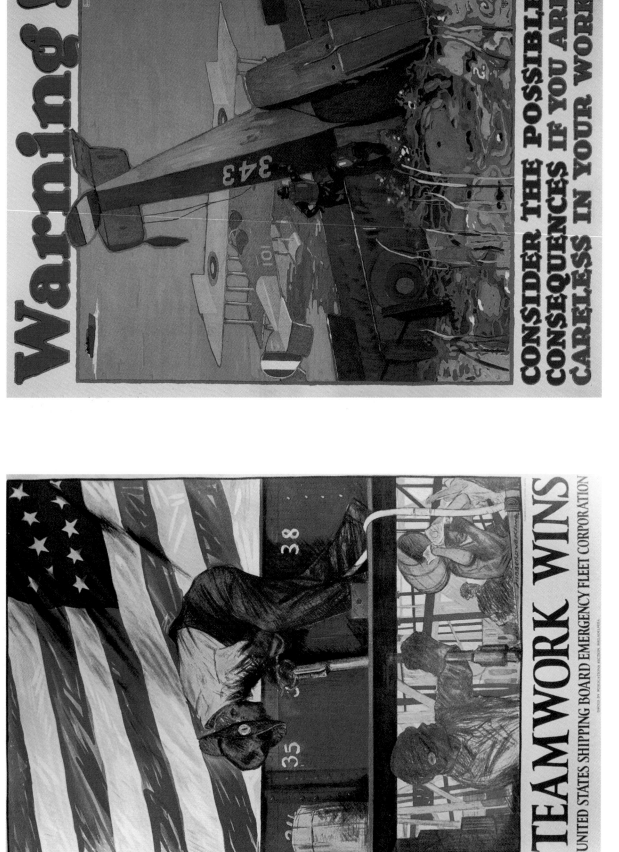

060. L. N. Britton, c. 1917

059. Hibberd V. B. Kline, c. 1918

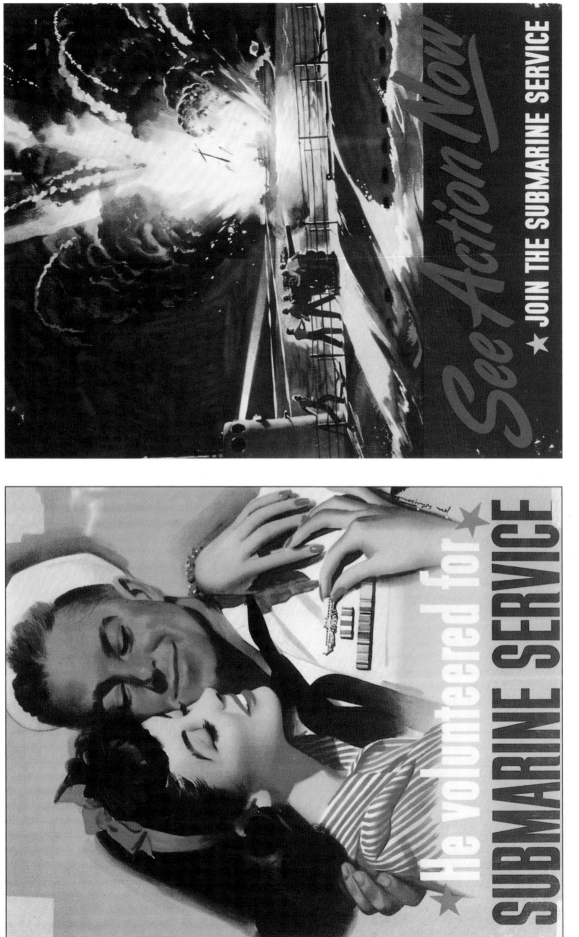

062. ARTIST UNKNOWN, 1944

061. JON WHITCOMB, 1944

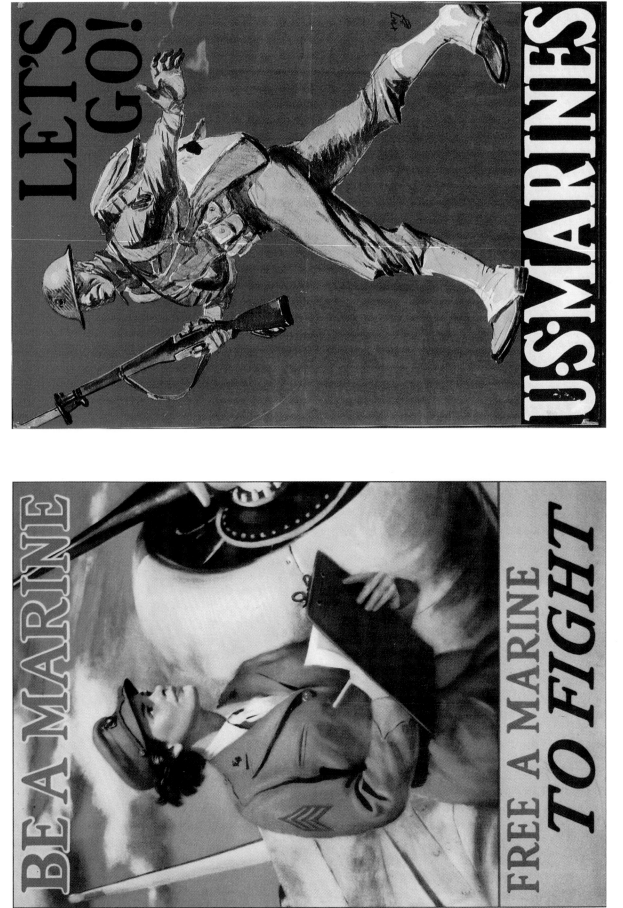

064. Artist Unknown, 1942

063. Artist Unknown, n.d.

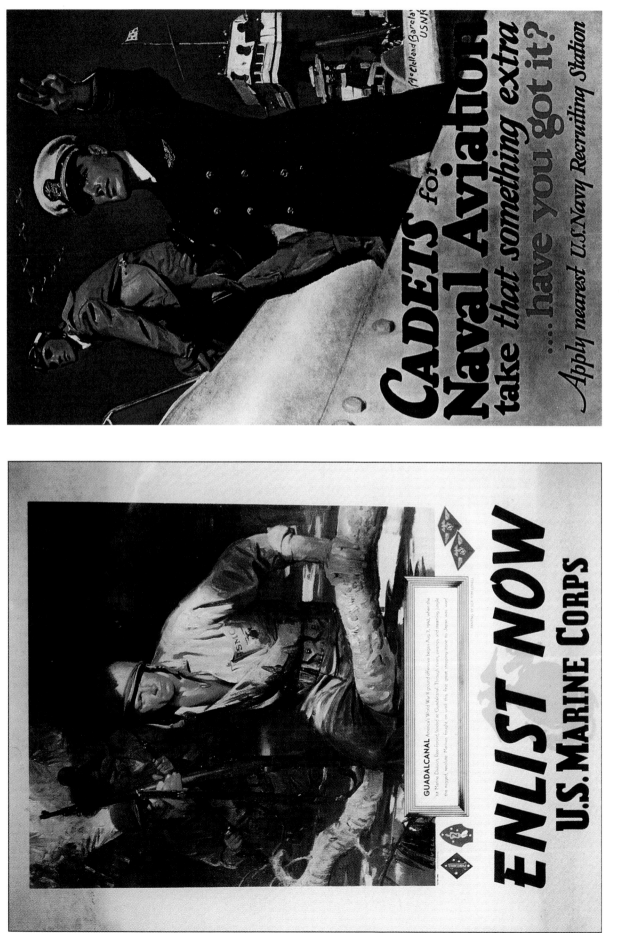

066. McClelland Barclay, n.d.

065. Sgt. Tom Lovell, 1945

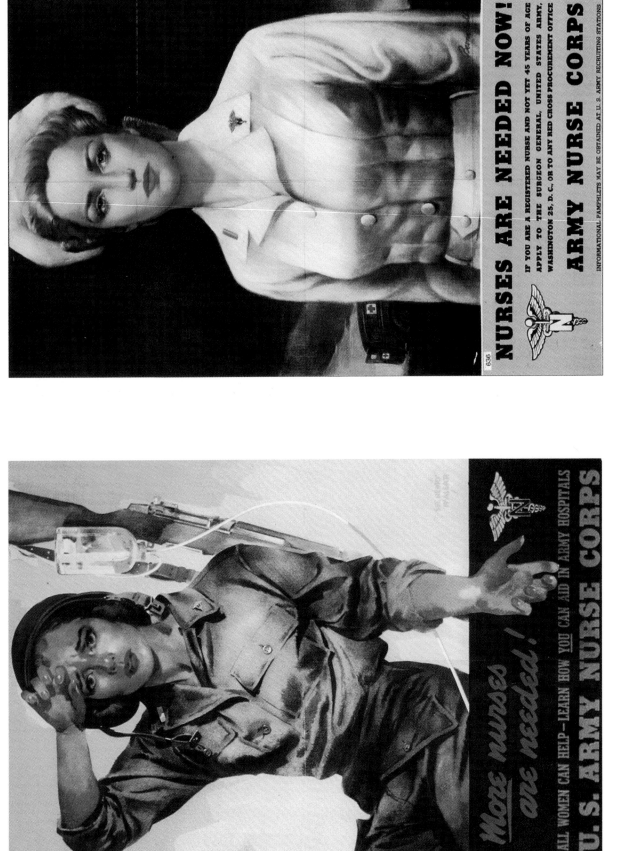

068. BERNATCHKE, 1945

067. SGT. HENRY McALEAR, 1944

070. MARTHA SAWYERS, 1944

069. H. H. WILKINSONS, 1942

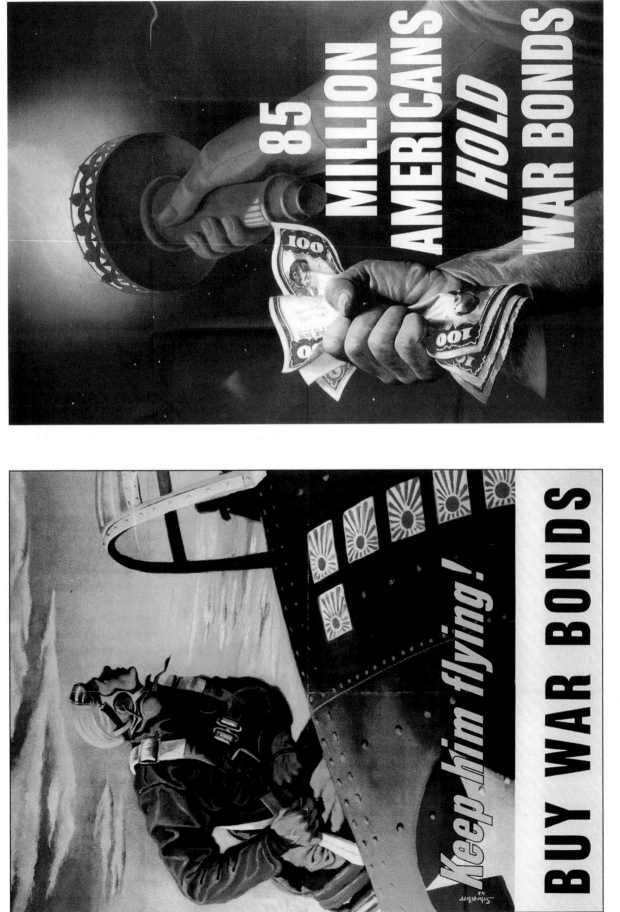

072. Melbourne Brindle, 1945

071. George Schreiber, 1942

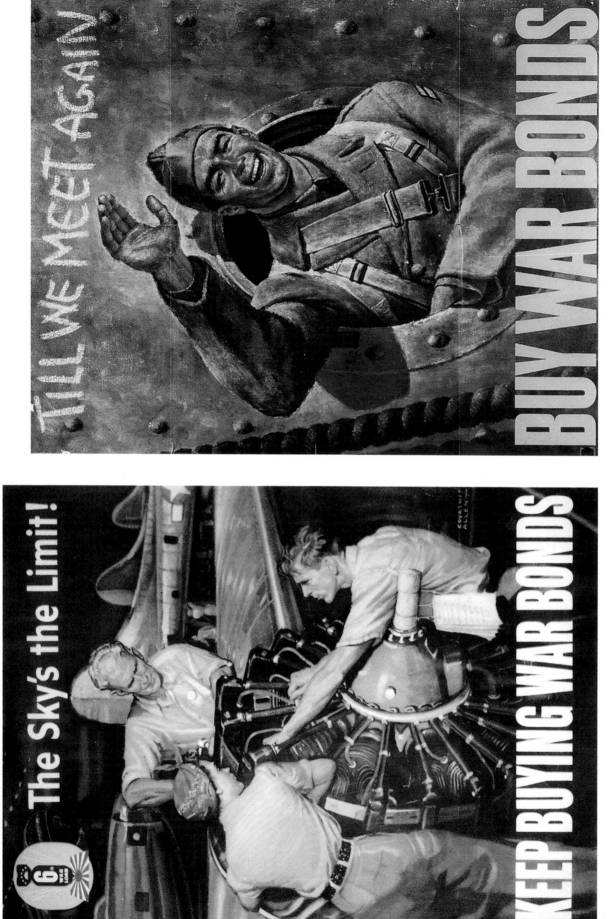

074. ARTIST UNKNOWN, 1942

073. COURTNEY ALLEN, 1944

076. Vic Guinnell, n.d.

075. Bernard Perlin, 1943

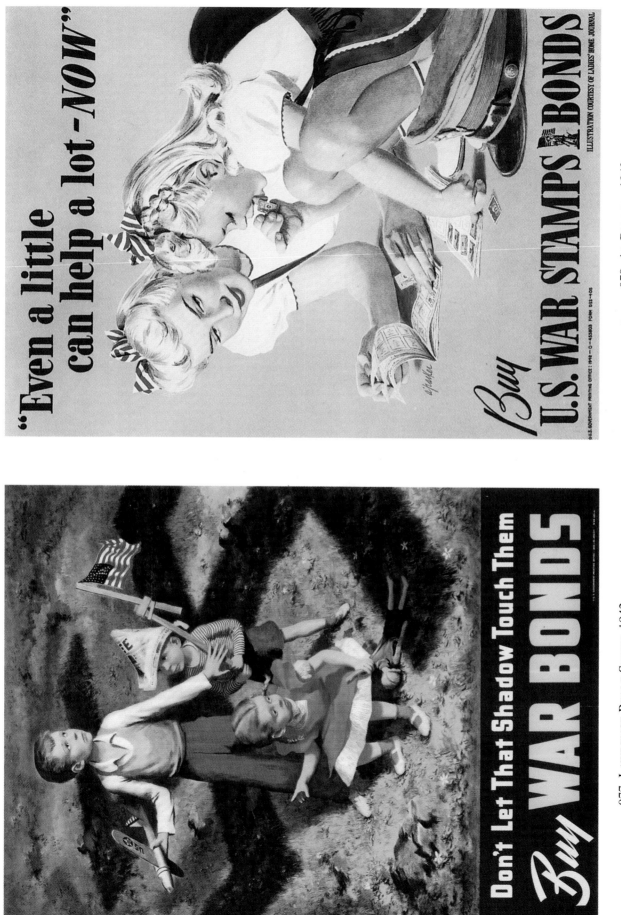

078. AL PARKER, 1942

077. LAWRENCE BEALE SMITH, 1942

They're fighting harder than ever

are you buying MORE WAR BONDS THAN EVER?

OFFICIAL U.S. TREASURY POSTER

080. HEWITT, N.D.

BACK 'EM UP

BUY EXTRA BONDS

079. BORIS CHALIAPIN, 1944

082. Dean Cornwell, 1945

081. Bingham, 1944

CARE is costly

BUY WAR BONDS & STAMPS

084. Adolph Treidler, 1945

NOW..ALL TOGETHER

7th WAR LOAN

083. Cecil Calvert Beall, 1945

086. ANTON OTTO FISCHER, 1942

085. ANTON OTTO FISCHER, 1943

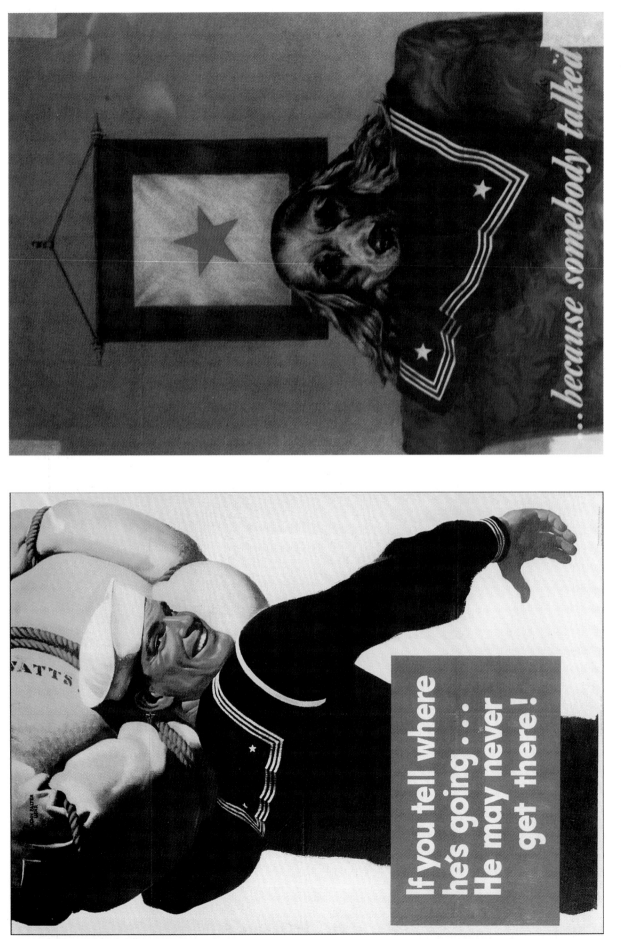

088. WESLEY HEYMAN, 1944

087. JOHN FALTER, 1943

090. J. Howard Miller, c. 1942

089. Essargee, n.d.

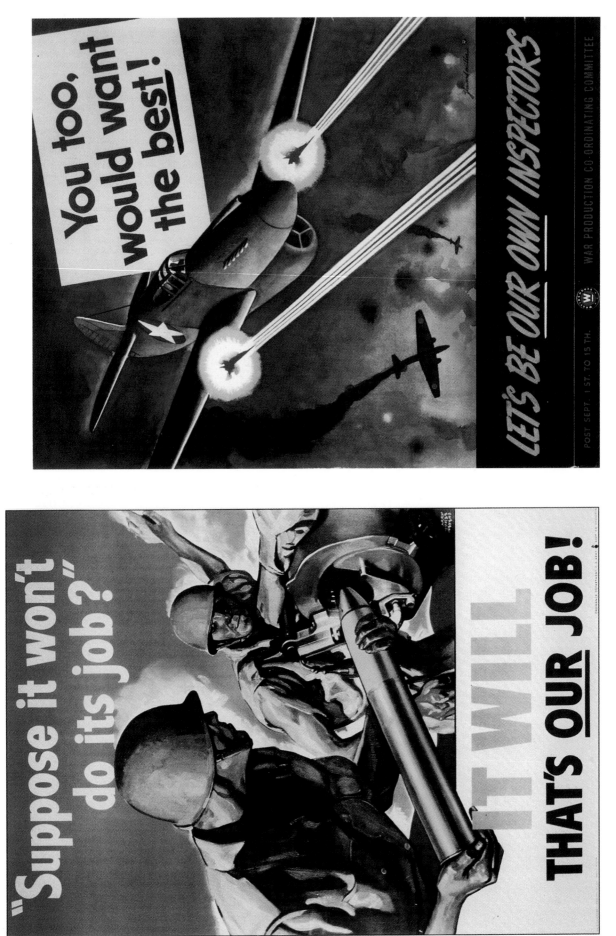

092. J. HOWARD MILLER, N.D.

091. HARRY MORSE MEYERS, 1942

094. Artist Unknown, n.d.

093. J. Howard Miller, n.d.

096. Artist Unknown, 1942

095. McClelland Barclay, 1942

098. John Falter, 1942

097. Artist Unknown, N.D.

100. E. R. WARD, 1942

099. HOWARD SCOTT, 1943

102. Artist Unknown, 1943

101. Artist Unknown, 1942

104. Valentino Sarra, 1943

103. Harry Morse Meyers, 1943

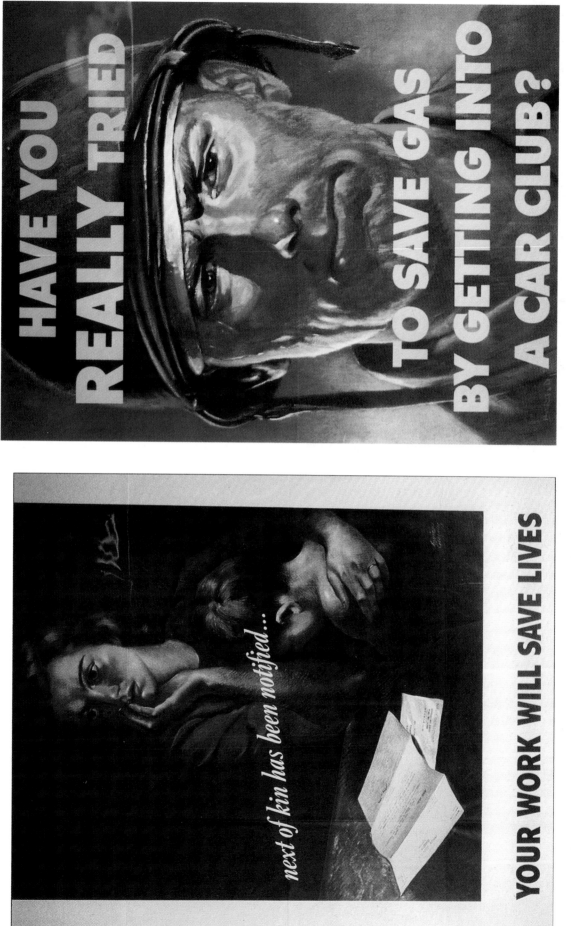

106. Harold Von Schmidt, 1944

105. Xavier Gonzalez, N.D.

108. Francis Criss, 1943

107. Artist Unknown, 1943

110. Perelli, 1942

109. McClelland Barclay, n.d.

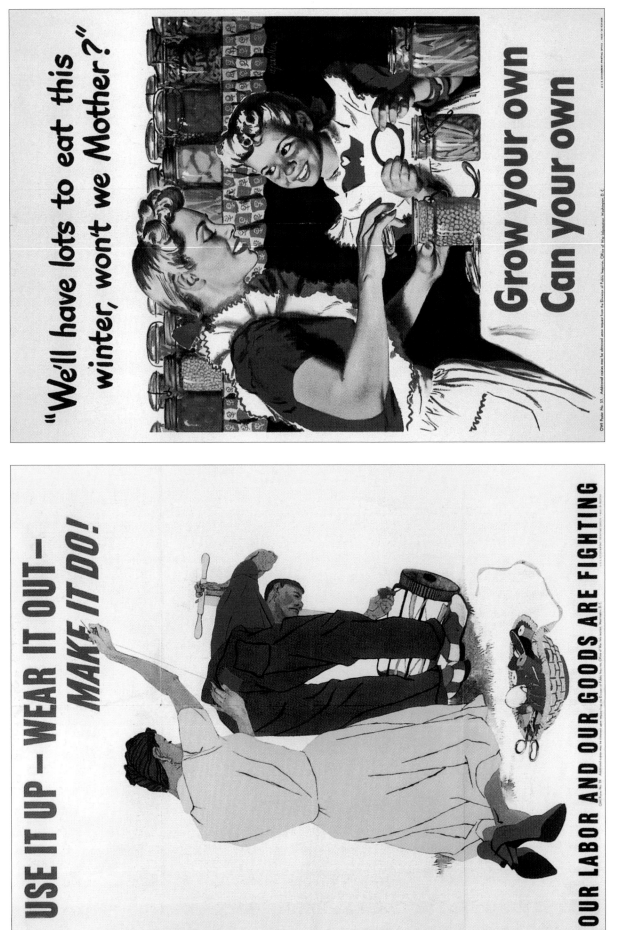

112. AL PARKER, 1943

111. ARTIST UNKNOWN, 1943

114. Artist Unknown, 1943

113. Morgan Douglas, 1943

116. Bernard Perlin and David Stone Martin, 1943

115. Artist Unknown, 1944

118. DAVID STONE MARTIN, 1943

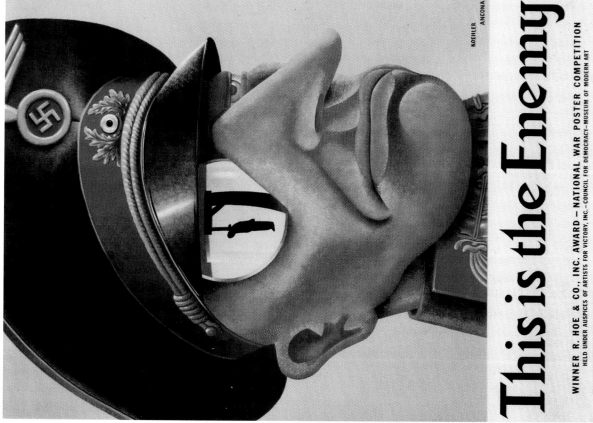

117. KARL KOEHLER AND VICTOR ANCONA, 1942

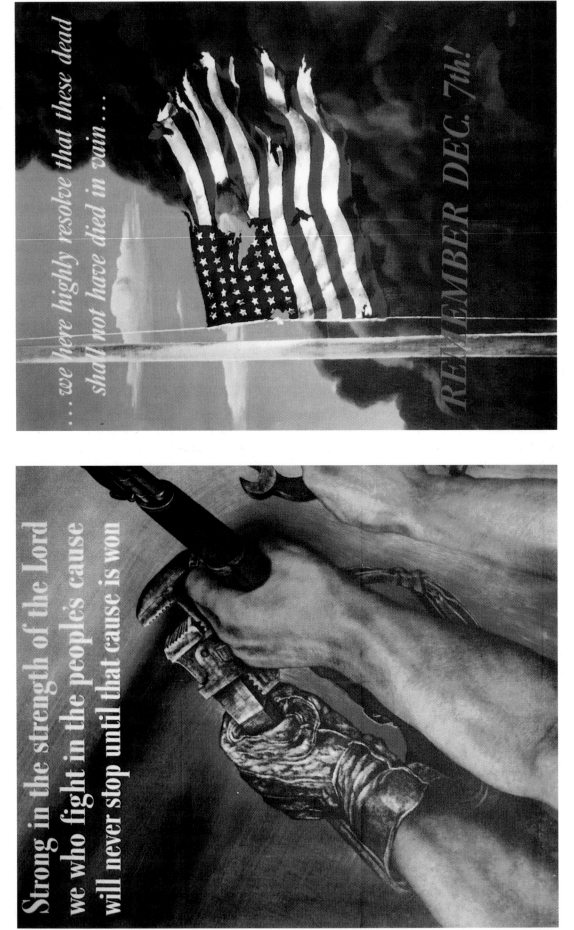

...we here highly resolve that these dead shall not have died in vain...

REMEMBER DEC. 7th!

120. Allen Russel Saalburg, 1942

Strong in the strength of the Lord we who fight in the people's cause will never stop until that cause is won

119. David Stone Martin, 1942

Alphabetical List of Artists